How to Get
a Golf Scholarship
to Stanford

A Parent's Guide

Richard P. Sinay

To Brian: For your dedication to
getting that Scholarship to Stanford

Preface

"Golf is a good walk, spoiled."

Mark Twain

Although Mark Twain may not have been the writer of the quote above, I like it anyway because it sounds like him. There is nothing spoiled about writing a book about how to get a kid to earn a scholarship to Stanford. It requires living the experience before one can write about it. I was one of those lucky parents with a kid devoted to achieving a golf scholarship at Stanford. It was not an easy task to achieve, yet it was not the intent right from the start of my son's golf life. He did not learn about Stanford until he was in the sixth grade, and that was in 1991. When my son decided to work to earn a scholarship to Stanford, golf was already pretty important in his life but there were no goals for it. He was not one who decided at a young age that he wanted to be a PGA Tour player. When he decided he wanted to play golf at Stanford, I just pushed him to follow his dream and did my best to guide him to that destination.

I wrote this for parents to show what the commitment is for them to make a goal like that accomplishable. I wrote it to impart the wisdom of what I learned from having experienced this and to prevent parents from making the same mistakes. I wrote it because it was fun reflecting on that period when we made that happen and knowing all the joy that it brought. I wrote it for my son, Brian, who made all the effort to make this goal achievable.

I hope readers find this beneficial to get your kid on the road to Stanford golf.

Introduction

"I wish I would have gone one more year at Stanford."

Tiger Woods

What parent doesn't want their child to go to Stanford? Whether they get there academically or athletically, it's one of the world's top five schools. My wife and I were lucky to have our son get to Stanford, and he wanted to go there when he learned about the college in the sixth grade.

Both the ladies' and men's golf programs are outstanding at Stanford. It is a gateway to the professional ranks as much as any college, and it is an outstanding academic school as well. Here are a few must-knows about getting to Stanford on a golf scholarship.

The first thing for parents to understand is that it is not easy. The child who wants to achieve that goal must be highly motivated both athletically and academically. He or she must work hard on the game of golf and very hard on the academic side. They have to be good enough to be offered a scholarship by the golf programs, and they have to be successful in the classroom in order to ensure their success in college. A player is not any good to a college who does not think they can handle the rigor of the college environment.

Stanford is the premier college athletic program in the country and a top-five academic school. Stanford has won the NACDA Directors' Cup for twenty-five years straight but recently had the streak broken by the University of Texas. The award is given to the top athletic college in the country for Divisions I, II, and II, as well as the NAIA and NJCAA. Points are awarded for high finishes in all sports, and the college with the most points in both men's and women's sports wins the award. This award, presented by the National Association of Collegiate Directors of Athletics, is prestigious.

The college received 55,471 applications for admission into Stanford for the fall of 2022 and a graduating class of 2025. The acceptance rate was just 3.95%, which was an all-time low for the university. There are not a lot of students who are accepted to enter these prestigious halls. Only 2,190 students obtained admission for the class of 2025. However, these numbers are based on academic access and do not include those accepted by athletic scholarships. However, getting accepted in the athletic program is equally as challenging.

This book is about getting into Stanford by way of golf. It is not as challenging to be taken into a sports program as it is to be accepted academically, but it is still not easy. The athlete must be good academically and athletically. The athlete does not have to have 1600 on the SATs or have a 4.5-grade point average; instead, they need to be outstanding students who manage the rigors of the Stanford curriculum.

Tiger Woods said that one of the most challenging things he did in college was achieving the academic requirements of his courses at Stanford. Undergraduate courses are a requirement for all students before they take the courses for their respective majors. Accomplishing those courses is a challenge, and these courses were what Tiger was talking about when he went to school there. He did not do a major because he dropped out after his first two years to play on the PGA Tour. He wished he had stayed for another year, but he would have had to declare a major and work for a degree in some subject area.

As one may assume, there are majors that athletes are "encouraged" to take. My son was encouraged to take the economics major because it wasn't too challenging and most athletes could manage it. There are majors of a like nature to choose from, and the golf coach will let the players know which might be the least challenging. However, the first two years of school are challenging enough because they require the student-athlete to pass each course to stay eligible for athletic competition.

I once had a student in my English class who was a gifted softball pitcher. I had to tell the parents that she needed to spend more time working on her books. Her father responded, "She doesn't need to worry about that because she's getting a scholarship." I indicated to him that a scholarship is intended to pay for the player's schooling. Athletic contribution to performance is still something the athlete must be responsible for, so preparing academically for college is mandatory. She got her scholarship to an excellent university but failed to maintain it because of academic nonperformance.

Another player that my son competed against as a junior was not academically capable. He only lasted one year at the college to which he received a full scholarship because he could not perform in the classroom. A more significant mistake was made by another golfer who was recruited to play for Stanford but turned down the scholarship to attend another college because some pros had made it to the PGA Tour from that college. He turned down the scholarship to Stanford because he thought he could make it to the PGA Tour from the other school. He did not make it to the tour because he went to that other school. I guess the player had never heard of Tiger Woods or Tom Watson and several others who are now playing on the tour from Stanford. Besides that, a degree from Stanford is a lot better for one's future than a degree from a much lesser-known college. Stanford is a community of people who take care of each other. Without making it to the PGA Tour, a player's college degree is quite important.

Another thing to realize is that the preparation for going to Stanford begins right away, even before the child is born. That's right. In this book, I will immediately indicate what a parent can do to help give the child an academic advantage. There must be as much effort in the academic realm as there is for golf. This makes being admitted to Stanford on a golf scholarship quite challenging. Playing the game of golf and improving one's golf skills is highly time-consuming, so doing well academically further enhances the challenge. So both aspects of what is required to be successful start almost immediately after the child is born.

A significant part of the book will show the importance of several aspects of being successful at golf. This book will deal with the importance of joining and playing at a country club, the need to play in many golf tournaments, the physical preparation of the player, the demands for practice by the player, the need for excellent instruction, and the decision as to whether the parent should coach the child.

There will also be a discussion about academic preparation, including the need to prepare for the Scholastic Aptitude Test. Stanford demands a minimum performance to enter as an athlete. Academic preparation is as necessary as athletic preparation because that is really what a scholarship to Stanford is. I will show what it takes to accomplish that requirement.

Throughout the book, I will include stories of many accomplished players, including Sergio Garcia, Hunter Mahan, Kevin Na, John Merrick, Sean O'Hair, and others. They all came across our paths as we went around the country playing in golf tournaments or here in Southern California. These future great golfers were at golf tournaments when my son was a player. And, of course, there will be stories about Tiger Woods since he also attended Stanford, and we will learn something from his attendance at that school. I am pleased to present a guide for getting your son or daughter to play golf at Stanford and receive an outstanding education.

Chapter 1: Early Academic and Athletic Beginnings

"Golf, like the measles, should be caught young, for, if postponed to riper years, the results may be serious."

P.G. Wodehouse

All parents want their children to be successful in school. There is a lot to say about early childhood education, which begins before the child is born. I can discuss this because I managed to earn a master's degree in reading. This degree taught me the importance of reading to the child, and studies show that reading to the child before they are born gives the child a several-month lead on the acquisition of language. Success in school is highly dependent on the ability of the child to read. Reading to the child is more important than any activity one can perform before entrance into school. My wife and I read to our two children from the early stages of pregnancy until they were in the second or third grade. Both were outstanding students right from the beginning of their schooling. Surrounding children with books is essential to getting off to a great start in school.

Early success in school means later success in school. This success pattern remains the same unless there is some dramatic change in the family dynamics. An additional and more meaningful activity a parent can take is allowing the child to be the oldest in their class. A Harvard-Yale study indicated that eighty percent of all athletic and academic scholarships go to the most senior students in the class. We started our children in kindergarten at six years old, the boy turning six before he began and the girl turning six just a month into school. August and September are the ideal months for children to be born. They will be the oldest in the class if they start kindergarten at age six. Both managed to get straight As throughout school. There are those teachers who thought no one should get an A grade. My son had one, so he got one "B" from her.

My experience as an educator and parent led me to this understanding. What happens in elementary school is a precursor to what happens in junior high school, and junior high school is an indication of what happens in high school. In short, early success in school leads to overall success in school. Their success is the main reason for wanting to make the child the oldest in the class. They have two opportunities to be successful: athletically because of their physical maturity and academically because of their social maturity. Parents must take advantage of the studies that have already shown that later registration to school is better than early registration.

In my case, I was just seventeen when I graduated from high school and a whole month away from being eighteen. Both my academics and athletics were affected by the fact that I had just turned five years old when I entered kindergarten. A whole year of more physical and emotional maturity would have been incredible for my growth. Some states recognize these vast differences in performance between the oldest and the youngest. They are adjusting to help the younger students by isolating them in different classes for their instruction. A study by the National Bureau of Economic Affairs concluded "that children who enter school when they are older do better academically than those who turn five right before the beginning of the school year." (Dhuey, et al August, 2017)

Aside from the early academic beginnings, there is the golf side of the preparation. I have several stories to share with the reader about what kind of competition there is in this sport. For instance, Tiger Woods is a classic example of a player who grew up hitting a whiffle ball with his little plastic club and walking around in diapers doing this. His father, Earl, indicated that Tiger watched him hit balls for about three years sitting in a highchair. Earl said that Tiger "internalized" the swing just by watching him hit balls into the net in his garage. Earl was a good golfer so the model of his swing was good enough for Tiger to internalize.

We have all seen Tiger's son, Charley, hitting, chipping, pitching, and putting golf balls, and he is a mini-Tiger. He mimics his movements, and he mimics everything he does. Each year, a golf tournament featuring fathers and sons shows how children mimic their parents.

Phil Mickelson, who was five years older than Tiger, watched his dad chip golf balls, but ironically did a "mirror image" of his dad and started chipping balls with the club left-handed. He just modeled after his dad but from the left side. That is how Mickelson, a right-hander in everything else, learned to hit left-handed. Modeling is the power of imaging. The child will model the parent's actions if you are a good golfer. Because Phil's dad was a good player, the model was worthwhile. If you as a parent are not a good golfer, then many videos of great golf swings are something to use to imbue a good golf swing in your kid.

There are stories of other prodigies starting out hitting a plastic golf ball with a plastic club: Rory McIlroy, Justin Thomas, and Jordan Speith, to name a few. Each of these players had early beginnings with a golf swing. My son was the same in his very early years, going around the house whacking at a whiffle ball and doing so in the backyard when he got good at it. It is just the foundation of the golf swing. It is what many of the best players in the modern era have done, so it is wise to allow the child to do so. It is all about making it fun, relaxing, and enjoyable.

Ernie Els and Phil Mickelson had chipping and putting greens in their backyards, though this may not be economically feasible for most parents. I had very tight grass in the backyard that allowed for putting and chipping, so my son practiced there before we went to the golf course. Young players at ages three, four, and five are good to do a moderate amount of short game actively at home in those early years. It teaches the player feel, and it teaches them to learn the coordination of the body to hit the ball properly.

Learning to play golf is not the only sport to engage in. Jack Nicklaus grew up learning to play all kinds of sports, which certainly did not hurt his performance when he became an adult. So, it is essential to teach the child how to play baseball, basketball, and tennis to help with the hand eye coordination. With competition being what it is, it might be okay to limit the time playing other sports, but it is not recommended that one give up all other sports, at least for those early years. Other sports teach the kid to be team players, and they learn to socialize better with others. It is best for your kid to learn team sports as well. Your kid will get off to a good start if they begin the game early and they learn to read before they enter school. Performing in other sports at a young age will give them the hand eye coordination necessary for a successful beginning.

Chapter 2: A Parent as Golf Coach

"Dad, now that I'm older, I have a better idea of everything you did for me when I was growing up. You worked hard to make sure I was happy and healthy and had everything I needed…I don't think I'll ever be able to thank your enough for all you've done for me, but, today and always, please know how grateful I am."

Anonymous

Although there is no ironclad rule about whether a parent should be the teacher and coach of a young golfer, the general sentiment is that they should not be doing that job. There are exceptions to this rule as I will discuss in this chapter but putting oneself in that position could have long-term negative consequences. Let's look at the different possibilities before making a judgment about this vital task.

There are many success stories about parents playing the role of teacher of golf and the coach of their sons or daughters. Jim Furyk, a highly successful player on the PGA Tour, has always had his dad, Mike Furyk, as his teacher and coach. Mike was an assistant pro at Edgemont Country Club and eventually the head professional at Fayette County's Uniontown Country Club. The two of them obviously have had a great relationship and they have managed to stay together through all the successes of Jim's career.

Another example of a successful relationship is that of Sergio Garcia and his father, Victor Garcia. The success they have had is heralded. Even though Sergio did not win as many majors as he was capable of doing, he is a Master's champion, and he won many tournaments on the PGA Tour and the European Tour. Sergio's father is a club pro, and an accomplished player himself. He was a highly respected professional in Spain for many years and competed successfully on the European Senior Tour for several years. The career that Sergio had can be attributed to the hard work his dad put in.

A very successful father-son team is that of Justin and Mike Thomas. They managed a close relationship despite Mike being Justin's coach from the very get-go. In fact, one can still see Mike teaching and directing his son during many of the current golf tournaments. Justin is a two-time major champion. Mike was a successful golfer (and his father Paul Thomas was as well) and so Justin had a wonderful foundation for growing up with the game of golf. Just remember that they are all professionals teaching their children.

Certainly, the reader has seen the likes of Charlie Woods, the son of Tiger Woods, play golf. Charley is on his way to becoming a very good player on the junior circuit and I am sure he will be a pro one day. His swing is the spitting image of his dad. He mimics all his dad's moves and demonstrates outstanding skills. Just keep in mind that as a parent who does not have the skills of Tiger Woods, this is the kind of competition one is up against.

Throughout the history of golf, there have been children of excellent players who have become successful themselves because of the teaching of their parent, who was a professional player. There have also been a lot of failures in that regard as well. Despite being the best player to ever play the game, Jack Nicklaus did not have a highly successful son as a golfer unless one thinks that making it to the PGA Tour is highly successful. Making it there and winning are two different things. Making it there and making enough money to stay on the tour is also necessary to retain the players tour card.

A couple of Jack's sons were outstanding players but not good enough to make a living out of it. Having a successful parent on the PGA Tour does not guarantee success for the child. Gary Player had the same experience of not putting forward a son who could play as well as he did or even come close. Good instruction from a great playing dad does not always equal success. Sometimes living in the shadow of a great player is more of a detriment than it is an asset.

So prospective parents and teachers of your son or daughter, this is the competition that you have when trying to play coach and teacher of your young golfer. This is not to discourage you from trying to make your young golfer a successful one on the PGA Tour. But my warning is to make you aware of the level of understanding that these players have about the game of golf and that trying to "compete" with their level of understanding is impossible. Therefore, it is highly recommended that the parents have very good professional help right from the beginning of the young golfer's career. For the early part of the young player's life, The First Tee is a good foundational start for the young golfer. In addition to that, the young golfer can get short-game instruction from a very qualified instructor in the immediate area. It is very important that the instructor has significant credentials before subjecting the young golfer to instruction that is not up to quality standards.

There have been parents who coached their kids only to have it turn out to be a disaster. This issue not only applies to golf but to many other sports as well. Sometimes the parent just wants to live their life through the young player. Sometimes they just want to get the kid to be successful so they can reap the rewards of that success. This was the case with Mark O'Hair, the father of Sean O'Hair, a very successful player on the PGA Tour. Their relationship ended in estrangement because of the overbearing behavior of the father. It is a well-known story, one that was captured on a *60 Minutes* episode.

After playing on the American Junior Golf Association (AJGA) circuit during his teen years, Mark forced his son to quit high school and begin playing on the Nationwide Tour, the minor leagues of golf at the time, at the age of seventeen to recoup his "investment" in his son. The result was horrific. Sean did not make but two cuts in the seventeen tournaments he played in, and that failure ended the relationship between Sean and his father.

There were great disagreements and Mark and Sean had some altercations. During the time that Sean was playing on the junior circuit, if he failed to do well, Mark forced him to run a great distance as punishment for his lack of success. Perhaps the irony of all this is that Sean later said that the strict discipline had prepared him to be successful on the PGA tour. Although Sean admits that several of the things that his father taught him were good, he does not agree that all of it was right.

Even though Mark O'Hair was not an accomplished golfer, he "invested" a great deal of money in preparing his son to be a PGA Tour player instead of teaching Sean himself. Mark sent Sean to the Bradenton School of Golf in Bradenton, Florida, at the cost of forty thousand dollars per year to get him prepared to be a player on the tour. However, his overbearing dad was eventually rejected when Sean initially failed as a player, but separation allowed Sean to demonstrate his skills at a very high level. He is still currently doing well on the PGA Tour.

Another player who was taught by his dad was James Oh, a competitor against my son during his junior amateur years. James was taught and taken around the country competing with the best in the country in junior tournaments. After winning the USGA Junior Amateur, James had a bright future ahead of him. But after only one year at the University of Nevada at Las Vegas, James tried out for the PGA Tour qualifying school and didn't make it. He played on the Nationwide Tour for several years but was only able to win one tournament and eventually lost his card. He eventually became a short-game teacher and is highly successful.

Another Dad who threw big money behind his son was Monte Mahan, the father of Hunter Mahan. He took Hunter to Texas to work with Hank Haney, a renowned, superb golf instructor. Hunter became an All-American and a very successful player on the PGA Tour. This is a case where great golf instruction from a superb golf instructor paid off. Monte rolled the dice for his son and the great instruction allowed Hunter to have a very successful PGA Tour career.

It was the same for another player that my son played with and that was Kevin Na. Kevin's father was said to have taken his son to Butch Harmon to get a golf swing and his success was assured by that instruction. Many things happened to Kevin before he found his swing and managed to overcome his demons before becoming a highly successful player on the PGA Tour.

Another dad who spent a lot of time teaching his son was Earl Woods, the father of Tiger Woods. As you have constantly heard over the years, the praise that Tiger gives to his father is extraordinary. One wonders if that praise was given because Tiger's public relations people didn't want him to say negative things about some of his father's behavior. Earl was also a strict disciplinarian, and it has been documented that if he thought Tiger was not giving his best effort out on the course, he would personally go out there, grab him by the ear, and pull him off the golf course. There were several disciplinary things Earl would do to help prepare him for the PGA Tour. It is without a doubt that Earl's strong discipline got Tiger to dig in and work hard (as he has said many times) enough to believe he was outworking the other players. (This, by the way, was the same thing Ben Hogan said, "I just outworked my fellow competition.") Tiger did the same, but he had a dad who was quite tough on him.

Earl was a good golfer, but he did not have the level of knowledge about the game that Tiger needed to maximize his success. Tiger had a teacher at a very young age and one that stuck with him throughout his childhood years from ages four to ten. His name was Rudy Duran. Although he taught Tiger excellent fundamentals, it would not be until after Tiger won the Masters by twelve shots that he would seek one of the top instructors in the country, Butch Harmon. That was in 1996 when Tiger was just twenty-one, the youngest winner of the Masters.

There are also those dads who were successful that knew very little about golf and learned the game as they taught their sons. The first example of this kind of relationship is between Xander Schauffele and his father Stephan, who was an Olympic athlete for Germany. It would be later when the family moved to San Diego that Stephan would take up golf instruction and then start teaching his son at the age of twelve how to play golf. It was not a perfect combination, but the explosive fire of their two personalities managed to work out. Xander has become a star on the PGA Tour. At the time of this writing, he is leading the BMW tournament with one day remaining and the elimination of an additional forty players to round out the finalists for the FedEx Cup, a ten-million-dollar prize to the winner.

It is best in my view to leave the instruction of the young golfer to the professionals. Trying to be a coach/parent instructing your young player is not a good thing. It is a waste of time. If a young player gets good instruction from the beginning from competent instructors, then that is the best way to go. Trying to take the shortcut and competing with the likes of parents who are far more knowledgeable and competent to teach golf is far too challenging.

Chapter 3: Coaching
My Son to Stanford

"When I see you out on the golf course all the time
with your son, I am just amazed at the dedication you
have for him. It is incredibly gratifying to see that and
I just want you to know how I view your effort."

Newport Beach Country Club Member

I consider myself the dad who did not know much about golf
when my son was young, but I managed to get him to Stanford
on a golf scholarship. I was a busy person teaching full-time
at the high school and part-time at the community colleges
near me. The best part was having the summers off so I could
take him to golf tournaments and help improve his game and
mine as well. In the early going, the instruction I gave him
was picked up from the books I read. When Brian was old
enough to understand the instruction, he took lessons from a
country club pro. It was not the best instruction because most
country club pros don't have the time to devote to the learning
necessary to be a top-rated instructor.

My son was learning from an early age just as we have heard about the most successful golfers like Tiger Woods, Rory McIlroy, Justin Thomas, and Jordan Speith. Brian started just the same. He had all the plastic golf clubs and he had his little putter. He spent a lot of time "playing" the game in the backyard. Learning the feel of the game at an early age will pay dividends in the long run. I had him on the greens at the local golf club at an early age just putting and chipping. I did not teach the swing at an early age because he was just learning it naturally by swinging his plastic golf club. He was probably six or seven when he started hitting real golf balls, but he had whacked around that whiffle ball many times as a very young kid. He already had a swing.

I taught him the fundamentals of setup, grip, posture, and ball position when he first started hitting real golf balls. Hitting the golf ball successfully requires good fundamentals. It is important that the young golfer has success right from the beginning. Golf can be quite frustrating if one does not start successfully. Therefore, making sure that the fundamentals are followed allows a young player to experience success from the very beginning. I used to rummage through the range and pick up golf balls players left by other players because they left for their tee time. Hitting a lot of golf balls is not as important as knowing how to hit them.

By the time Brian was nine years old, he had played many rounds of golf at Dove Canyon Country Club. So, it was time for him to enter his first tournament. We drove out to Borrego Springs in an area east of San Diego and Brian teed it up in a howling wind for nine holes and shot a 42. He won the tournament in the eleven and under category. This would prove to be highly motivational for him. He won the second golf tournament he played in. Having early success is what motivates a young player to work harder on the game.

What I am indicating here is the importance of having success early. It is very motivational for the kid golfer. He has a trophy in his hands, and he managed to do it all by himself. (Well, did dad help?). Of course, I was so proud of him and how he managed this howling wind and got the ball into the hole better than the several other competitors that were there. Winning is a magical motivator. If the young player is ready, then success is guaranteed.Without detailing his junior golf career, (the reader can see that in my other book *Who We Met on the Way to Stanford: A Father's Memoir*) I will just indicate why Stanford became the focus of Brian's desire as a golfer. When Brian was about twelve years old, he and his friend Steve Conway were talking about going to college and Steve told Brian that his dad went to Stanford. Brian didn't know about Stanford because Tiger had not even arrived there yet, so Steve told him all about it. Before the end of Steve's description, Brian had decided that he wanted to go there. Before long, he was wearing a Stanford sweatshirt to school.

The summer after his sixth-grade year, he played in the San Diego Junior World tournament for the third time. It was the 11-12 division played at Pine Glenn golf course in the San Diego area. There were three rounds of golf and Brian came out the winner. It was a very big deal to win a golf tournament that Tiger Woods had won at the age of twelve.

It was shortly after that I encouraged Brian to write a letter to the golf coach at Stanford and tell him that he would like to play for him at Stanford. I had read an article indicating that Tiger had done so at the urging of his father. And so, Brian sent off the letter.

Sometime during the remainder of the summer, Wally Goodwin showed up at a tournament to watch Brian play golf. He introduced himself and thus began a friendship that would last for six more years. Throughout the years that Brian played golf at tournaments across the country or in his home state, Wally would be there from time to time to say hello. He was a wonderful fellow who had coached at Stanford for many years and was coaching Tiger at the time he was recruiting Brian and other players. So, Tiger and Brian sent a letter to the golf coach at Stanford. It is not a problem to do this.

Brian continued to improve because of his total dedication to the sport. At the age of twelve, Brian decided that playing soccer, baseball, and golf was too much so he gave all his attention to golf. Winning a major junior tournament catapulted his motivation. Brian's goal was to get to Stanford and play golf.

When Brian was a freshman in high school in 1997, the Southern California High School Championships were played at Canyon Country Club in Palm Springs. They had been playing there for quite a few years; it's where Tiger Woods set the record for the lowest score in that championship in his junior year with a 67. The pins were in the same place for the one-day tournament and in the sweltering heat of 105 degrees F, the players who represented 586 high schools came to battle it out for the first-place trophy.

It was a tortuous six-hour round of golf, and in the end, Brian won the tournament with a three under par 69. It was quite a feat for a freshman. Tiger and a few others had done it. This victory put him on the sports page of the *LA Times* and he gained a great deal of notoriety for this accomplishment. Wally Goodwin took note and came the following year to watch the tournament. Brian finished in the top five in his sophomore year. It was another great showing in a very difficult competition.

The same tournament two years later would solidify Brian's scholarship to Stanford. In the 1999 tournament of the

Southern California High school championships, Brian would shoot a 65 and beat Tiger Woods' record by one stroke. Brian again was champion of 586 high schools in Southern California.

That was in late May of 1999, and by July 1st of that summer, Wally Goodwin offered him a golf scholarship during a phone conversation. Brian had achieved his dream of going to college at Stanford University and playing for the college team. It was a dream come true for him. It was his dream, one that was accomplished with a lot of hard work and a lot of support from his dad.

During the time Brian played golf in the summers of his fifth through eleventh grade years, there were tournaments all over the country. He won over thirty local tournaments in different age groups. He started traveling to tournaments when he was a freshman in high school at about fifteen years old.

His performances at these national tournaments were always good. He was always in the top twenty or closer. His consistent performance was enough of an indication to the coach at Stanford that he would continue to develop as a player. Coach Goodwin said when he arrived at Stanford that Brian would be the next NCAA College Champion from Stanford. He had the ability to do that.

The gist of this chapter is to point out that contacting the coach and showing interest in playing golf at Stanford is a good thing to do. The young player must be doing well and the following chapters are the ways to get that accomplished.

Chapter 4: Joining a Country Club

"They call it golf because all the other
four-letter words were taken."

Ray Floyd

We all know that Jack Nicklaus grew up playing golf at a country club in Columbus, Ohio. Even though he played many sports as a kid, he devoted himself to golf at an early age at Scioto Country Club. I once saw the schedule that he kept honing his skills as a player with his teacher Jack Grout. During the summers he practiced all day. He would take a break for lunch but get right back to work hitting golf balls until late into the day. If there is one thing sure about practicing at a country club, it is the chance to do it for as long as one likes. Even though joining a country club is advantageous, it is not mandatory. There are excellent golfers from both sides of the golf world.

Nicklaus had two great things going for him as he developed as a player at that golf course. He had access to the golf course, and he had a great teacher of the game. He was way ahead of all those other players who tried to knock him off his pedestal during the late '50s, 60s, 70s, and '80s. Jack won his sixth Green Jacket at the age of forty-six in 1986. And so, it is incumbent upon any parent who wants their young golfer to start out with an advantage to join a country club.

Even though it is recommended that one does this, it has not always been mandatory for success. The greatest example of someone who was not raised at a country club is Tiger Woods. A close second would be Lee Trevino. Neither had the "benefit" of growing up at a country club like Tom Kite and Ben Crenshaw who honed their skills at Austin Country Club. The difference is the ability of the parents to afford that luxury. If they do not have the means to join the country club, then they must rely on what is available to them. In Tiger's case, his father was a veteran so he had access to the naval base golf course in Los Alamitos. CA. Tiger also played at Heartwell Golf Course and El Dorado Park in Long Beach.

At the Navy course at Los Alamitos, there is a nine-hole course and an eighteen-hole course that Tiger played as he grew up. Lee Trevino also grew up playing wherever he could, first becoming a caddy at the Dallas Athletic Club, then learning to play golf while he was in the Marines. So, success can come to those who come from the public golf course but a country club beginning is pretty standard today.

Joining the country club has several important advantages for the parent. The club pros will watch over the kid when he is there practicing. The young golfer can get lunch at the club, and practice at the facilities as much as necessary. If the player is as fortunate as Jack Nicklaus, the teacher of his golf swing will be a resident pro. This was unfortunately one of the missing elements of my son's training. None of the members of the club at either Dove Canyon Country Club or at Newport Beach Country Club were of a status significant enough to teach him a good golf swing. Despite being good players, they were not good teachers at the club. And so, his early instruction was a bit shaky.

Although he had very good fundamental skills, he was not getting an excellent education from any of the teachers he had. In the meantime, other players that he grew up with were getting better instruction. Belonging to a country club does not guarantee access to the best golf teachers so I had to find someone who could teach him well. Because I was not aware of the complexities of the golf swing; I did not seek out the very best instructors because they were either too far away or too expensive. I read the books of the best instructors: Harmon, Ledbetter, and Haney, but that is not quite the same as working with them. Therefore, in the long run, the ability to have the country club give him the necessary time to play and develop was not enough to make him the great player he could have become.

The bottom line is that there are many clubs around the country that have outstanding instructors. Young players during my son's day went to them and took lessons from some of the best teachers in the country. As I have said, Hunter Mahan went to Hank Haney and Kevin Na had a stint with Butch Harmon, and Charles Howell worked directly with David Ledbetter. Other players that Brian played with did not seek out the highest levels of instruction but still managed to play on the PGA Tour. John Merrick was one of them. He had a successful stint on the PGA Tour after graduating from UCLA. He was also a public golf player and did not belong to a country club.

Even though it is highly recommended that the player belongs to a country club, it is not mandatory for success. However, it is a distinct advantage to have that facility always available to play and practice. At a public facility, one is always having to work around all the other people who want the same space. There is more freedom at a country club. The ability to play a lot of golf is a distinct advantage to making your young player successful.

What is more important: practice or playing time? Hogan used to say that once he was done practicing, he would take his skills to the golf course. It isn't anything to consistently hit the ball on the driving range if you cannot duplicate it on the golf course. That is the advantage of the country club. You can test the learning one has done on the range and apply it to the golf course. Hank Haney has said that Tiger Woods was the most remarkable range player he has ever seen. He could hit perfect shots time after time after time on the driving range only to find himself not doing so on the golf course. In Tiger's earlier days as a player, he earned the name Woods, because he found himself in them quite often. It was making these mistakes that got him to learn how to negotiate his way out of trouble. He could hit five of them in the woods and still manage to make a par or even birdie on a hole. It was the mistake of not hitting the ball on the golf course as successfully as he had done on the range that made him the remarkable player that he became. So, taking the game to the golf course is something that one can do if one belongs to the country club.

A player becomes better with time invested. The more time invested, the better the player becomes if there is good instruction mixed into the pot. Time invested is what gives the player the ability to know different shots and experience different situations that allow them to mature as a player. For instance, reading greens on a golf course is as much experiential as anything else. Country club play is an opportunity for the young golfer to gain experience playing the game and learning the nuances of it.

My son had the advantage of playing old and having the opportunity to play at Dove Canyon Country Club from eight years old until about ten was exceptionally helpful. The practice facilities at this club were stellar and it was a foundation builder to be able to practice out of outstanding bunkers and great chipping greens. After that, he was able to play at Newport Beach Country Club, a place much closer to our home. It afforded him the opportunity to get to the course, practice, and come home in a relatively short period of time. The only issue with Newport at the time was that there wasn't a good place to practice sand play. It took doing it on the golf course to learn effective techniques. However, the greens were quite good, and the putting facility was excellent.

Newport Beach Country Club began supporting the Champions Tour starting in 1995; it was called the Hoag Classic. The benefit to the membership was the conditioning of the golf course so that it was in excellent shape for the tournament. My son was not only able to benefit from that but seeing some of the great players perform was quite valuable. He was able to meet some of the best players ever: Jack Nicklaus, Gary Player, and others. For him, joining a country club was not only beneficial for the game but also for his inspiration.

Chapter 5: The Reality of Practice

"There isn't enough daylight in any one day to practice all the shots you need to." and "Every day that I missed practicing takes me one day longer to be good."

Ben Hogan

It is well known that two players who achieved greatness on the PGA Tour had a green and bunker in their backyards at home: Ernie Els and Phil Mickelson. While there may have been others who also did this, it is important to know that these two excelled in the short game. I am not recommending that parents set this kind of structure up for their prospective golfers, but I want to emphasize how important it is for young golfers to have the opportunity to hone their skills using some facility that is available to them.

A great deal of time must be put into the short game.

Developing the skills of the player comes from all the time invested. The more time invested in developing the skills, the "older" the golfer gets in skill levels of the various aspects of the golf game. There is not only time spent on hitting golf balls and developing the swing, but there is necessary time to spend on chipping, pitching, the sand game, and the all-important putting game. If one investigates the time and efforts of some of the great players, the reality is that many of them put in enormous amounts of time to achieve their skills. It is almost certain that a player will take the entire summer to develop their skills for each of the years leading up to competing in tournaments. Competing in tournaments is the goal of the early practice and play of the young golfer, and this will be discussed in another chapter.

Practicing golf should be done in a structured manner. There should be goals set while practicing for growth to take place. It is vitally important that the player uses the time wisely to improve the skills that he or she has already been taught.

While I was not a very good golfer at the time I was instructing my son, I was not nearly as informed as I could have been if I learned from my own practice. The professional lessons my son took were not on pitching, putting, sand play, or chipping and so I had to be the help for him to improve to a higher level of player. I read as many books as I could in the short game, but reading a book is not the same as having put in the time as a player. Sometimes one must learn through practice, but excellent instruction shortens the road to high achievement and discovering the nuances of each of those skills.

Today there are so many good short game gurus with James Oh being one of the best. He played a lot of junior golf with Brian. There is no doubt that learning some of these skills is experiential, but most of these skills can be learned from excellent instruction. Sometimes young golfers just figure out how to handle these different skills through experience. It's a matter of having them be able to practice these skills and find out what works and what doesn't. What parents need to realize is that the child needs to invest a great deal of time to develop these skills. Tiger has said that his dad told him that he had to outwork everyone to be sure that he would be competitive.

Chapter 6: Golf Instruction – The Long Game

"There are no absolutes in golf. Golf is such an individual game, and no two people's swings are alike."

Kathy Whitworth

Let me take a moment to reiterate the importance of good instruction. There are many levels of instructors out there. It is like a pyramid with the very best instructors at the top of the pyramid down to individuals who may be teaching at a local public course because they are looking to earn their PGA status.

There are several things to look for in a golf instructor you want your player to work with. First, they should have a zero handicap or better. Anyone who has accomplished that level of golf has put a great deal of time into the game. Secondly, they should know about the swings of the very best golfers like Hogan, Snead, Player, and Woods. They should teach the player using video equipment that compares their student's swings with the best players in the world. They should also have a high level of knowledge about the short game. The instructor should be fair and reasonable about the cost if your golfer is young versus more advanced in age and ability.

Golf instruction can be started as early as three years old. There have been many players who were swinging a plastic golf club when they were just out of diapers: Tiger Woods, Rory McIlroy, Justin Thomas, and Brian Sinay among others. I put my own kid in there because he had that little plastic golf club and a plastic ball, and he went whacking away at it when he was three. We had a nice backyard then and he hit it like he was swinging a hockey stick. It was good training, and it was a good beginning. It was what some of the great players of our time have done as well.

Despite these early beginnings of great players, there is no ironclad rule about when golf instruction should begin. Sometimes too early can lead to burnout unless the kid is incredibly motivated. One should be cautious about too much too soon. There is no actual time when a young player should start swinging at golf balls. Very good players on the PGA Tour started very late in life and were quite successful. Perhaps this is not possible today because the competition levels have risen significantly. Getting early instruction is important but not as important as who you choose to do the instruction.

I did not get instruction for Brian until he was around ten years old. That was a mistake. He could have started earlier, but he didn't.

Golf instruction varies widely. By that I mean one can get very poor instruction from one professional and very good instruction from a different professional. A club pro can be a good golf instructor and they can be poor as well. What is it that one has to look for in a good golf instructor? What is their background, how many students have they taught, and how many professional players have they worked with? In the early stages of the young players' growth, it is very important for them to build good habits and those come from good golf instruction.

While my son worked with a club pro who got his reputation for teaching all the better young players in the local region, he was woefully inadequate as a teacher. Let me tell the reader why. I once asked him during his instruction of Brian how his wrists were supposed to act during the swing. His answer was something like "What wrists?" Or he implied there was nothing to know about what the wrists are supposed to do during a golf swing. As I write this, I know a great deal more than I did when he was instructing Brian, but it did not make sense to me that wrist movement did not have any part in the golf swing. I think he got defensive because he didn't know the answer, I was asking questions of him, and he felt offended by them because he was the "golf professional" and I was just an English teacher. Well, an English teacher who reads. I had read David Leadbetter's book *The Golf Swing*.

I was shocked and dismayed. Although I did not know what the wrists were supposed to be doing during the golf swing, I had seen Tiger Woods at the San Diego Open, the LA Open, and other professionals at The Bob Hope Classic using the hell out of their powerful wrists when they hit a golf ball. Once, standing directly behind the likes of Arnold Palmer who was about to hit a drive, Arnie cranked those wrists and hit the hell out of the ball straight down the middle! He turned and looked at me and winked as I was aghast at how far he had hit it! And to illustrate the point further, when Jack Nicklaus came to Dove Canyon Country Club to dedicate the course (as he had done with all his courses, he built by playing an inaugural round), Jack found himself stuck about thirty yards right behind a tree on the left side of the fairway of a Par 5. Since we members were able to follow the players closely on the fairway, I was within earshot of Jack and asked, "Who put that tree there?" Everyone who heard the comment laughed and Jack said, "What tree?" With 250 yards of distance to cover the green, Jack pulled out a five-wood, and lined himself up to hit the ball through the "Y" in the tree! He set up, turned, and fired. Right through the tree the ball sailed up in the air and landed about two yards off the green to the right of the pin!

The point is that when he hit that ball, the dexterity of his hands and wrists was paramount in that shot. Great players are gifted with great hands. Jack used those deft hands on the greens and won himself eighteen majors. So, when my son was working with this popular club pro who had nothing to say about the use of the wrists when hitting the golf ball, my son lost time in improving his game. Today, as I write this, I know that wrist movement is central to striking a golf ball. There is a lot of very good instruction out there so research it first before committing the kid to it.

The one caveat to getting quality golf instruction is that it costs more. It is why I went the "cheap" route because it was not in the budget to hire a top-notch teaching pro. It is better to take fewer lessons from a top-notch teaching pro than to take a bunch of misleading lessons from a club pro. Club pros are not necessarily great golf instructors. Good golf instructors have to intensely study the golf swing and it takes a lot of hours to do that. A club pro does not have that kind of time. A club pro relies on the instruction he got himself as a player oftentimes. Even a professional golfer is not necessarily the best person to teach someone golf. I learned that when my son was at Stanford. The coach was a former PGA Tour player, but he was not a very good instructor.

Here is my recommendation. In the early years of a young player, it is as important to have a high-level instructor as it is in the teen years and late teens. First, let's look at the story of Hunter Mahan. Hunter was one year behind Brian playing junior golf in Southern California. Junior golf was run by the Southern California Junior Golf Association, and they divided the players by age groups: 11 and under played by the red tees; 12-13 played by the white tees; 14-15 from the blue tees; and 16-18 from the back tees. Hunter was playing in the 11 and under group and he had to compete against three players that were the same age but several months older than him. The three players were Brian Sinay, Steve Conway, and James Oh. James Oh was the premier player at the time, but the victories in junior golf tournaments around Southern California were shared by the three players. At one time after a significant tournament, Hunter had finished fourth behind the three greedy winners. I said to him, "Hunter, you keep working on that short game, and you are going to find yourself winning down the road." I said it to be nice and because he was such a great kid, I wanted him to win.

Before long, Hunter's dad, Monte Hunter, decided to move to Texas and take his son to get instructed by Hank Haney. I had heard of Hank Haney as a golf instructor but what could we do living in Southern California when Hank taught golf at a facility near Dallas, Texas?

But Monte was determined to make Hunter a good golfer and so he sold his California house and used the money to get the very best instruction for Hunter.

It would pay off. Hunter would win the 1999 5A Texas State High School Golf Championship and the 1999 U.S. Junior Amateur. Comparatively, my son Brian would win the Southern California High School Championships (583 high schools) with a round of 65 and set the high school record set by Tiger Woods. Tiger won the Southern California High School Championships three times, one of three players to do so. Hunter's skills had improved dramatically after working with Hank Haney. As some of the readers may know, Hunter went on to be an All-American at Oklahoma State and then had a very fine PGA Tour career before losing his game. Eventually, a player's accomplishments are going to be better with great instruction.

More directly, another player who my son played with in tournaments was Charles Howell. He has made a great living being in the top ten of many tournaments in his career. He has not won a lot of tournaments but winning 40 million dollars in winnings is enough to keep many people comfortable. Again, Charles was a student of David Ledbetter and developed a terrific swing that has done him well. The point of this is to say that players who are instructed at the highest levels do well.

Another player who was just two years younger than Brian was Kevin Na. He is another example of a player who went to the best instructor, in his case Butch Harmon, and developed a swing that has netted him millions, though I cannot confirm that Butch Harmon was solely responsible for his improved golf swing.

While there are many lesser-known names who are great teachers of the game of golf, it is important not to waste time on instructors who do not have appropriate credentials. Another instructor that my son spent time with was Donnie Hill, the former Angel baseball player. The problem with working with him was that Donnie was a student of the game at the time he was instructing my son. He may have had some idea as to what to do to manage a good swing, but my son ended up with behaviors in his swing that hurt him instead of helping him. In short, instead of learning to shallow the swing, (because Donnie Hill did not know about this), my son continued to swing too steeply, and it hurt his distance. By the time he got to college, he was being outdistanced by smaller players who had better swings that came more from the inside than over the top. They had better swings because they had better instructors.

Obviously one of the problems with accessing these top-level instructors is the cost and their proximity. If you live in another state, then the only way to get that instructor is to move near where they are. Since that is not always possible, unless the parents want to take that kind of risk (and many have), then the best road to take is to research the nearest best instructor to the proximity of where one lives. It is best to leave poor instructors alone and save money. If they offer a cheap deal, then they are certainly not good. The parent must research this and find out from the local PGA who the best instructors are for the region one is living in.

Excellent instruction has been made available to parents online with some great instructors: there are several sources that can be accessed for a nominal fee. Let me give some of my recommendations: Clay Ballard's Top Speed Golf and Performance Golf. The bottom line is that the best instructors will produce the best results.

Chapter 7: Golf Instruction – The Short Game

"The more I practice, the luckier I get."

Gary Player

Phil Mickelson and Ernie Els competed against each other in the San Diego Junior World golf tournament as kids. Both came to the tournament with sharp short games because they had a green and a sand trap in the backyard of their houses when they were growing up. Learning how to manipulate the golf ball is a matter of trial and error, and there are different ways to go about it. Severino Ballesteros used the oceanfront beach as his training ground with one club and a couple of balls and he learned how to hit every conceivable shot with that club. Tiger Woods did all his early learning at local public golf courses. He was not a country club boy like Jack Nicklaus, Tom Kite, and Ben Crenshaw. Whatever the venue is, a player must spend a good deal of time honing the short game. There are four separate skills to master: putting, chipping, pitching, and sand play.

A putting green is always available at the local public golf course. Before we joined a country club, we spent a lot of time at the local putting green. The young player's putter needs to be adjusted for their height. This allows the young golfer to stand in the correct posture for putting. This is important so the young player can develop the proper posture and arm and shoulder movement right from the beginning. It is quite important to establish the right posture for putting. Randomly slapping around a golf ball with an oversized putter is a waste of time. I have seen that too often. It is not doing the golfer much good to practice hitting a golf ball without addressing it properly. This does not mean it will take the fun out of the player's time on the greens. Better posture and address will make them successful and that is what needs to be seen.

Learning the right technique for chipping and putting right from the early days of learning both skills is more important than anything. It is not a matter of just how much time one puts into the game, but how much quality time is applied to the game. Quality time is time spent using the correct technique when practicing the skill. There are a lot of subtleties that a player learns from good instruction. Today more than ever, there are outstanding instructors online to teach the subtleties of the short game. This is why the level of competition gets more and more difficult each year.

Learning to play out of sand is quite important as well. I suggest reading Gary Player's *Bunker Play* because it is the Bible of sand play. Read this over and over to learn from perhaps the greatest sand player of all time. Gary Player was a guy who, like Hogan, dug the answers of how to play shots "out of the dirt." In this case, out of the sand. Some of the stories of his incredible accomplishments as a golfer are in the book along with his great instruction. As a parent, it is best to read this to assist the young player who rarely gets a lesson in sand play. Mr. Gary Player demonstrates all the answers in the book.

Learning all the short game shots takes time, but the time is shortened when the right techniques are learned before practicing. Players who did not have the benefit of short game instruction in another era learned from trial and error, though there were books written by players who could articulate the instruction like Hogan's *Five Lessons*, Bobby Jones's *On Golf,* and Horton Smith's *The Secrets of Putting* were all books the legendary players relied on for golf instruction. If you look at the style of putting that Jack Nicklaus and Horton Smith used, one can see a remarkable resemblance. Although I am referring to instruction during and before the time of Player, Nicklaus, and Palmer, one can be sure that their teachers were readers of those books.

Today there is a myriad of short game instructors like Dave Pelz who fashioned the short game of Phil Mickelson. Although some of these short-game instructors can be quite expensive, it is not uncommon for parents to spend tens of thousands of dollars for the best instruction. It is a gamble and one that pays off handsomely for some and not so well for others. I once had a dad tell me he spent one hundred thousand dollars for three years for each of his two girls at the Bradenton School of golf and neither one of them made it to the LPGA. It isn't always just the amount of money one pays, but also whether the player has all of the other tools to compete at the highest levels.

What are the tools needed to play at the highest levels of golf? I cannot speak to them as an expert because I just have my ideas about what I learned. It takes a great deal of concentration to be a great player. The mind cannot be easily distracted. It is not a game for people who have attention deficit disorder. They cannot focus long enough to make it through eighteen holes without their minds going somewhere else.

A second characteristic is an ability to be unaffected by a shot in golf whether it is a missed putt or a missed chip. Great players learn to control their emotions when playing at the highest levels. There have been players who had some success despite their temper like Tom Weiskopf. Yet, it has been said that had he not had a temper, he may have done as well as Nicklaus. Bobby Jones succeeded despite having a terrible temper, one that had him throw his club over the heads of people in the gallery. Tiger Woods was also no saint when it came to controlling emotions with all the times he was fined for verbal misfires. But these people are rare because they manage to settle down quickly and get back to concentrating on the next shot. Sam Snead said, "I just let out a little steam and then go back to my game."

Winning golf tournaments comes down to a great short game and an excellent ability to putt. Putting is the most important skill followed by pitching then chipping and sand play. Each of these skills takes time to master. It is the amount of time and the amount of good practice that advances a player toward a successful career in golf.

Chapter 8: The Motivated Golfer

"The most important shot in golf is the next one."

Ben Hogan

There must be a reason why a young golfer is going to put in so much time to improve his game. Some players knew at an early age that they wanted to be a player on the PGA Tour. Three players that come to mind are Rory McIlroy, Jordan Speith, and Justin Thomas. Each of these players knew from an early age that they wanted to be golf professionals. Like any other profession, there are those who know what they want to do very young. But there are others who focus on the goal of getting a golf scholarship to earn a good education and play golf at the same time for their college. If the reader is so lucky as to have a son or daughter who is motivated to be on the PGA or LPGA, then they are just a wind-up doll running to get their goal accomplished. It is built-in motivation. They are not only obsessed but possessed with a desire to make themselves professional golfers. When looking at their careers and their early golf, they began very early, and they held onto that obsession with golf all the way to stardom. Becoming a star player is rare since many players do not know how they will perform when the pressure is on. Learning to deal with pressure comes from having the opportunity to be under pressure. All of that is accomplished when the player spends a lot of time playing in a competition.

Some players are motivated to earn the golf scholarship and leave it at that. My son learned about Stanford University in the sixth grade, and he became motivated to get to that college using golf. He was a smart kid, and smart enough to realize that achieving that goal academically was not possible for him. I suppose if he spent all his time working on his books, it might have been possible, but Stanford does not pick students just because they are academically talented. The selected students also possess unusual characteristics that set them apart from their peers like having the ability to play the violin at the concert level, performing in plays, or being a master at chess and other hobbies. They want people who are interesting and who can share their talents with others. That is partially how they are accepted in the academic realm.

Stanford also does not place students in type dormitories like most colleges. They do not put athletes with athletes in a dorm. My son got paired with computer students in his dorm, and eventually, the skill rubbed off on him. So how one is placed at the school may have an impact on what the kid wants to do once they get to the school. I once had a father complaining to me that his son was going to Stanford and taking a philosophy degree. He wanted him to study business because he was a business guy himself. Such is life.

In the meantime, the more he learned about Stanford, the more motivated he was to get there. This was the driving force for his hard work on his golf game. He was never practicing his golf game because he was interested in becoming a PGA Tour player. His goal was to get to Stanford, play golf there, and get an excellent education. And because that was his goal, it was achieved. A young person has to have a lot of motivation to accomplish the goal of playing well enough to get a scholarship to Stanford.

The first thing to realize about a young golfer is that his motivation is his or her own. It is not the parents that motivate the young golfer. Motivation is internal. A player can't be "paid" to be motivated. It is usually there because the player wants to achieve whatever goal they have set. In my son's junior year of high school, he had worked particularly hard on his game because the summer after his junior year, he would hear from Wally Goodwin about an offer to play at Stanford. Wally had his eyes set on three players that he felt could bring the next NCAA championship to Stanford. They were Travis Whisman from Nevada, Jim Seki from Hawaii, and Brian Sinay from California. Travis and Jim had their eyes set on becoming professional golfers. Brian had his eyes on getting to Stanford. Their ultimate motivations were different.

I had taken Brian to the tournament and watched him warm up and said to him that his swing really looked good. I was not going to follow him as he played for reasons I will explain in another chapter, probably at the end of this book. In any case, it was the usual shotgun start and off Brian went on hole number three at Canyon Country Club in Palm Springs.

After three holes of playing, Brian was two under par, and on his way to the fourth hole, he stepped over to me and said, "Dad, I think you want to watch me play today. I'm going to play pretty well." And so, I followed him for the next fifteen holes, and it was just a thing of beauty. Drives were right down the middle, with irons on the greens and close to the holes. After seventeen holes of play, he was seven under par. A large group of people had heard that this performance was going on and all the writers for different papers were there taking notes as he went from hole to hole. When he reached the last hole of the day, it was par five and his drive was perfect. The second shot left him a tiny wedge into the green and he hit it to four feet or so. It was a relatively short putt. However, he missed the putt and parred the hole for a round of 65, two strokes better than Tiger Woods' record, set at the same golf course several years earlier. The head pro had heard that a young man was tearing up the golf course and came out to watch his performance. He came over to me and said, "Congratulations, Dad. The pin placements for this tournament have been the same for the many years we have held the tournament, so you should be proud that Brian performed at a higher level than Tiger Woods."

I was naturally excited to hear this story, but I knew that my son was no Tiger Woods. Tiger had won two US Junior Amateur tournaments at the same age as Brian and four Junior World tournaments. Brian had reached the quarterfinals at two US Juniors but never a semi-final match. He had done quite well in tournaments but not at Tiger's level. So, when we went back to the clubhouse and while we were walking, I asked Brian if he loved what he had done. His comment told me that he was not in love with golf. He said it was "okay." He was not so excited that he was the winner of a major high school championship that he just wanted to bust with pride. He accepted the trophy with great humility, and it was then that I knew he had no intention of making golf his life. It was not what he wanted. I am sure at the time that he did not know what he wanted to do with his life, but it was most certainly not going to be endless hitting of golf balls. To be sure, the victory sealed his ticket to Stanford. The golf coach came to the CIF Team finals in Lompoc at La Purisima Golf Course to touch base with Brian and congratulate him on his high school championship victory.

Brian sustained his motivation in his senior year and finished fifth at the high school championships. He had already been offered his scholarship by Wally and we had taken a trip to Stanford to be shown around by the coach. This was in the summer after his junior year before school started. It was his dream to get to see the campus and look at the golf facilities and learn the structure of how things would go while he was there. During our trip up there, Wally increased the scholarship by ten percent. Players can get as much as a one hundred percent scholarship down to partial scholarships. If a player manages to get into Stanford by other means, they can walk onto the team. That was done during the time my son went to Stanford. Stanford University usually carries ten guys on the team but only five of them are consistently playing. The level of scholarship is also dependent on the need. Players who come from homes that have means are not likely to get a full scholarship. Whatever Wally was offering, we as parents were not going to object to it because we wanted our son to fulfill his dream of attending Stanford and playing golf for them.

The scholarship offer was very good, and he was on his way to Stanford after his senior year. His senior year was challenging because of the high school courses he had to take to get into Stanford. Also, he wanted to maintain his nearly straight-A average. He worked hard on his academics, and he worked hard on his game to prepare himself for play in the fall season of his freshman year. I tell all of this to make people realize that accomplishing a goal is the work of the young player, and the coach/parent can help to make that happen.

If a player is not motivated to work hard and if it is more

the wish of the parent than the child, it will be nothing but a disaster. A player can be motivated and yet be forced to do things the way of the coach/parent and that will have major consequences as well. There is nothing luckier than to have a kid who has a goal to get somewhere. I had taught many students who would not lift a finger to do their academic work, but I had the great fortune to have a child who worked extremely hard at accomplishing both academic and athletic goals. Mostly because he was motivated internally and not from the outside.

Chapter 9: Playing in Golf Tournaments

"There is golf, and there is tournament golf."

Ben Hogan

Playing tournament golf is quite essential to the development of a good player. After all, playing in college requires a lot of time competing in golf tournaments. There are eleven golf tournaments a player can play at the college level for most Division I teams. If they get to that level, players have many choices today. The parents should enter the player into junior tournaments when they are ready. And by ready, I don't mean they have to win the tournament. They should be able to finish the round of golf with it being a decent success, a situation that will discourage the player rather than motivate them.

The first step in tournament play is at the local level. In Southern California, the SCJPGA, or Southern California Junior Golf Association, has several tournaments throughout the year for players to compete. Most tournaments are in the summer, when a young player can compete several times a week for trophies at different golf courses. These tournaments are divided by age group, and each group is just two years in span. There are several tournaments for players eleven and under. The players play from the red tees at each golf course, and they play just nine holes. Players will come from all over Southern California and play in the tournament. Most of the time, the parents can follow their young golfers and watch them compete. There is usually a junior golf representative from the SCJPGA who will monitor the sometimes-erratic behavior of the golfer's parents and sometimes even the kid himself.

When your young golfer has had great success at the local level, it will be time to apply to play at the national level. The AJGA is the premier junior golf national circuit, and players who are 12-15 can play in the AJGA Junior All-Star Series. Before doing so, they must have earned Performance Stars. Performance Stars are based on the player's finishes in the state, regional, and national level junior tournaments and AJGA qualifiers and tournaments. W

hile a player may be playing at the local level tournaments set up by the Junior PGA in their region, it is also necessary for young players to play at the national level whenever a tournament is held.

The San Diego Junior World Tournament (the one Tiger won six different times) is currently a top national tournament each summer. Players start earlier than age 6, then 7-8, 9-10, 11-12, 13-14, and 15-17. So, a player can play in this tournament twelve times now!

My son Brian first played this tournament when he was ten and finished second. He then played as an eleven-year-old and finished in the top five. As a twelve-year-old, he won the tournament. This is an excellent international tournament for young golfers to enter. What is important is that playing on this international level and succeeding as well as he did gave him a status as a player for the national level, and that was playing for the AJGA organization. It was here that coaches came to watch players and try to sink their claws into them for their teams.

An additional plus to come out of playing the San Diego Junior World tournament was the fact that the Japanese had decided to take the top eight players from each age level and send them to Japan, all expenses paid by one parent, to play in a competitive tournament called the Japan Cup. The same age groups that the Junior World Tournament had would be honored at the Japan Cup.

Brian would qualify for the tournament for three years in a row, at ages ten, eleven, and twelve. This was a quality and outstanding experience. The Japanese were exceptional and gracious hosts. The tournaments occurred in August at a prominent country club (found on the internet) outside of Nagoya, Japan. All the significant corporations sponsored the tournament in Japan, and when the welcoming party was held, all the Presidents of the companies were there to greet the players. The lead sponsor gave a speech comparing golf to life and how there are many turns and twists in a game of golf, just like life. It was a festive party with the international players greeting the best junior Japanese players. At the first tournament in 1992, Brian sat near a young player named Lorena Ochoa. As the reader knows, she became one of the great players in the LPGA in her short career at that level.

Another crucial national golf competition is the Drive, Chip, and Putt competition by the people at Augusta Country Club to encourage young players to become golfers. This excellent competition allows the young player to measure their skills against players of their age, demonstrating three good skills to play the game of golf. This is a competition that any parent wants their child to be involved with so that they have the opportunity to perform in the finals on TV at Augusta National Country Club, with prominent golf professionals singing their praises as they win their division.

A significant national tournament that young players can play in is the Orange Optimist tournament in Florida at the Trump Nation Doral Resort and Spa for 2023. Thanks to the generosity of many fine golfers who followed and supported the golf of Brian Sinay, he was able to play in this tournament during the summer of his junior year in high school. Here, he had the fortune to play two rounds of golf with a young, brash player from Spain named Sergio Garcia.

Sergio had won nearly every junior tournament in his young career as a junior player, but he had not won the Orange Optimist tournament. Sergio made it his last junior tournament before he became an amateur player, and my son was in his group (with one other player from Thailand) for two rounds of golf.

The performance of the first two set up the last two rounds. During the first round of golf, Brian played well but ended up a couple or three strokes behind Sergio. At this time, I realized the difference between a well-instructed junior and one that could have been better instructed. I did so because the University of North Carolina Tarheels coach approached me and asked me if Brian would like to play at North Carolina. I told the coach that he had his mind set on attending Stanford from the time he was in the sixth grade. I then asked the coach what he could see made the difference between the length of their drives because Sergio was hitting the ball at least twenty to thirty yards longer than Brian.

The coach said Sergio has "lag" in his swing, and Brain does not. I did not know what lag was in all the lessons he had taken with his swing coaches; unfortunately, he had spent a lot of time swinging without it. It was then that it dawned on me that the instruction received was so mediocre that I had missed one of the fundamentals of a good swing. It would be something that would develop into a problem later. Suffice it to say that this was a great learning experience and one that I was fortunate to have during play at the national level.

Then there is the high school golf experience, playing for one's school in leagues against other high schools and then moving on to higher levels of team and individual competition. The high school experience is vitally important to a player's exposure to coaches around the country, especially from coaches at the local level. Coaches watched my son in regional and final competitions and asked if he wanted to play for UCLA, USC, Pepperdine, and a dozen other schools in the Southern California area. I had to say no to them because, as I had shown, Brian wanted to go to Stanford, and that was it. He had no other interest in playing for any other team, even though his scholarship at these other schools would have been better than Stanford's.

Finally, there are the USGA tournaments: the US Junior Amateur, the US Amateur, and the US Open. These outstanding national tournaments will get any player a great deal of notoriety. Playing in the US Junior Amateur is an opportunity to play against the best future players in the country and to measure one's skills against their own. Tiger managed to win three of these tournaments, the only one ever to do so, and Jordan Speith is the only one to have won the tournament twice. Surprisingly, Jack Nicklaus never won the US Junior Amateur but lost in a semi-final match as his best finish. There have been many players who have won this title, never to become even a good player on the PGA Tour, and there are several who succeeded quite well. It is important to note that this is an outstanding tournament if only one can qualify. Sometimes the qualifying is more complicated than the tournament itself.

The US Amateur is quite a difficult tournament for which to qualify. This tournament is dominated by college-level players who seek the golden ring with this title. Winning it is a ticket into the Masters, and the future of one's golf is almost guaranteed. Most players who win the US Amateur become good professionals, but not all make that grade. Those that do make outstanding players on the PGA Tour will have achieved great success at the amateur level. The North-South Amateur is an example of a tournament where one can gain points and then rank in the amateur standings. Players earning enough points through performance in these amateur tournaments will automatically qualify for the 312-player field for this tournament. There are qualifying tournaments throughout the country for the U.S. Amateur, and it requires finishing at the top in the local tournament to be included in the field of 312 players.

Once one arrives at the tournament, there are two days of stroke play before the top 64 compete in match play. The number one seed is pitted against the number sixty-four player, and the winner moves on to the next match. In a remarkable three-year period, Tiger Woods won the US Amateurs three times in a row, a feat not accomplished by anyone. If your young golfer is going to be a serious player, they must perform well in the US Amateur. The other amateur tournaments to play are the Western Amateur, the Northeast Amateur, the Pacific Coast Amateur, the Sunnehanna Amateur, and the Southern California Amateur.

Chapter 9: Playing in Golf Tournaments

For a player to be competitive at the collegiate level, a player needs to play golf in local tournaments, high school tournaments, national tournaments, and amateur tournaments to prepare for the high level of competition at the collegiate level.

Chapter 10: The Physical Skills of the Golfer

"I still push 350 pounds with my legs; I do hundreds and hundreds and hundreds of sit-ups, I run on the treadmill at 85 years old at 'max,' so my body is 50 years of age."

Gary Player

Gary Player looked at me, then at my son, and said, "Don't build up your upper body if you want to play golf well." I was in decent shape in 1996 when he said that, but I had worked out with heavy weights at the urging of my physical education teacher in college because he wanted me to go out for the football team. I was an idiot then and followed almost anybody's advice. At the time, I was far from golf becoming so crucial in my life. But apparently, it was advice that would go unheeded as my son bought an elliptical trainer to gain strength so he could hit the golf ball farther. These are some of the important aspects of good physical preparation for golf.

Gary Player was indicating the fact that good golfers (in

general) are those that have narrow upper bodies so that they can generate a lot of swing speed. A long, languid body produces a long, languid swing, which is necessary for the golfer who wants to create a lot of clubhead speed. Despite being just five foot six inches tall, Gary Player was so fit that hitting a golf ball a long way was due to his incredible fitness. He was the precursor for the modern-day player who uses fitness to hit the golf ball prodigious distances. He had strong hands, arms, and legs. The golf ball is hit from the ground up so the legs need to be strong. Running allows for gaining that strength as well as having good stamina walking eighteen holes a day for three or four days. It is standard to be very fit, a must for a good golfer.

Another important feature of the superior golfer is to have a great deal of flexibility. Sam Sneed, at the age of 45, was said to be able to kick his leg up to a ceiling and nearly hit it. Sam was one of the loosest players on the PGA Tour and had a great deal of longevity as a golfer because of it. His swing was poetry in motion. He was as loose as a goose!

There were other great players with similar flexibility: Tiger Woods, Phil Mickelson, Ernie Els, Ben Hogan, and many others. Flexibility is an essential physical feature for any player who wants to play well for a long time. I am sure there is no doubt that Bernard Langer works on his flexibility. For him to maintain a high level of performance for as many years as he has, his physical work in the gym allowed him to have that incredible longevity as a highly successful player. He has made history but there is no doubt that he has excellent flexibility, perhaps caused by his hard work in the gym. Learning to stay in shape and being flexible are two good starts for any player.

Aside from flexibility, the player must have strong hands and muscular arms. Hogan, Palmer, and Player's components look like they worked in the steel mill pounding on anvils.

Palmer's and Hogan's hands were big, allowing them to grip the club lightly but with great strength simultaneously. A good strength coach is necessary for the proper way to build muscle without compromising the golfer's body. If the parent wants to know what their young golfer's physical look will be, then just have them look at Mom and Dad. For the most part, kids will duplicate the size of their parents. Boys grow up like Dad, and girls grow up like Mom. That does not mean their personalities will be exactly like their parents'. It could be the opposite. The girl can have the dad's personality, and the boy can have the mother's personality.

It is also said that long arms are an asset as well. Ben Hogan had long arms. Long arms give the player a long arc in the swing, and the longer the arc, the greater the speed of the club-head at impact. When one looks at Ben Hogan's swing, one is amazed at the fluidity and the long arc developed by such a short man. Golf is not a tall man's game, and even though a few tall men developed a highly successful cannon of victories, there are fewer of them than average sized players although the height of a player is getting bigger. An ideal height is around six feet tall to six foot three today.

While I realize that a parent can't manufacture the physical features of their child on command, many things can be done through physical training that will make the player much more competitive because of the enhanced physical features. It is a standard that all players on the PGA Tour work out constantly to maintain their bodies to perform at a higher level. Through workouts and trial and error, you will learn this over time.

Chapter 11: The Mental
Side of the Game

"The game of golf is 90% mental and 10% physical."

Jack Nicklaus

Golf can get to the best of players. It is an enormously challenging mental game. That is something that is not for everyone and those very few who manage to sustain a living on the tour for a long time manage to master the six inches between their ears. Tom Weiskopf said that if he knew what was going on in Jack Nicklaus' head, he might have been a better golfer. What should go on in the head of a golfer?

First, a player needs to have control over the emotions. Players who are successful with the game are usually quite calm under pressure. It is what Hemingway said of the person who shows grace under pressure, the bullfighter who stands his ground as the bull charges after the red cape. One of the special talents of the great players is to remain calm in the most difficult of circumstances and that is to be able to make a putt when it is needed. We have seen over the years the great putting of Nicklaus and Woods in the most crucial situations while playing for the victory in a tournament. There are numerous examples of their performance under pressure, and all of it starts with a calm mind. Some say these players have ice running through their veins.

There are numerous books to read to improve the mindset of the young golfer: Golf is Not a Game of Perfect by Bob Rotella; Zen Golf by Joseph Parent; and Putting Out of Your Mind by Bob Rotella. All of these and many more are sources for the mental side of the game that a young player can read during the summer travels to golf tournaments. A good golfer is a student of the game and knowing the game means knowing the psychology of the game as well.

Confidence as a player is built with a good golf game. A player who has been taught well and who has learned from playing in a lot of different situations is much more likely to be successful than an unprepared player. It is like showing up for the exam and having studied the material. A person who prepares is less likely to be afraid and un-confident. A well-prepared player is ready to be successful when they arrive at the tournament. Recently a player who had not won for a long time on the PGA tour was being congratulated by his wife because he had worked so hard on his game. Winning takes a lot of preparation and effort before showing up to the tournament. Confidence comes from preparation.

I do not think that players need to have a shrink. I think that players develop their confidence by establishing a good game and that is all about hard work. There are numerous hours of playing and practicing that make players successful. I know of stories of players who were banned from golf for a year, and they came back with incredible gains in their game.

They were told that they could not play and their response was to prove to those who banned them that they were wrong.

I cannot think of a more important goal than gaining confidence in one's game. It is just hard work and time. The golfer gets older the more time they put into the effort of improving the skills of their game. Once, Gary Player said he would not go into dinner until he had holed out three shots from the bunker. The difficulty was that he had to hole all three of them in a row! How is that for dedication?

Chapter 12: Accomplishing the Academics

"For true success, it matters what our goals are.
And it matters how we go about attaining them.
The means are as important as the ends, and how
we get there is as important as where we go."

Old Tom Morris

For a scholarship to Stanford, the athlete must be an outstanding student. I know what it takes to be a great student, and there are several things that parents can do to facilitate better performance.

Aside from the master's degree in English, I earned a Master's in reading.

Reading is essential to any student's success, and it is crucial that they learn early. It is okay to read to the child before the child is born. My wife and I did this with our children, and studies have shown significant gains. I will not cite any studies on this matter because this is not an academic book. Reading simple material from time to time while the child is moving around is a good idea. Reading lullabies and the like is essential for learning sounds that will eventually be articulated.

More importantly, the first five years of a child's life are the opportunity for the parent to imbue a great deal of linguistic knowledge in a child by reading daily to them. While I realize that this may not seem like a realistic goal, it was one that we managed to do our best for both kids. Read to them every day. Let them take in the language and give them the linguistic start that will allow them to excel in school. It distinguishes one child from the next in school: their language level. Students who were not ready are at a significant disadvantage entering school. The school cannot make up for the first five years of neglect with reading. The student is already behind and will stay so unless there is a significant increase in reading at home. The school only has a given number of hours to improve the student's language; the house has considerable time to do so.

Just as important as reading to the child is allowing them to express themselves in conversation with the parent. Speaking in complete sentences, telling the child who they are and why they are, and using language that is not baby talk will develop the child's linguistic skills as well. Spend a lot of time communicating with the child. It will pay dividends in the long run because having a facility with language is what separates children when they first enter school. Parents who ignore this preparation find their children behind in school almost immediately and spend their school years trying to catch up.

The child can gain an additional advantage if they are the oldest class member. As I have indicated previously, a 20-year study by Harvard and Yale determined that eighty percent of all academic and athletic scholarships go to the most senior members of each graduating class. And so, knowing about this study and having had our kids tested to see how they were doing at age five, it was suggested that they both be "held back" and become the oldest members of their class, or at least on the more senior side. My son was born on August 21st, so he was six years old when he started kindergarten. This proved beneficial because he was considered an "old" freshman in high school, and he was physically big enough to play against all eighteen-year-olds in the high school championship. The reader will learn that Brian won the Southern California High School Championship at fifteen years and nine months. By the time he was a junior, playing in the same tournament, he was seventeen and nine months. He would win it for the second time in his junior year. He missed winning the same championship by a couple of strokes in his senior year, making just one mistake on the same course he had won two significant titles.

The young golfer must become a reader of books to increase the language level to deal with the complex challenges of high school. The home must be where mom and dad are readers because kids will model what their parents do. It is incumbent on the parent to show the reading by doing it themselves instead of ordering the child to read. Reading needs to be fun, and it needs to be what is talked about at the dinner table. Reading and sharing it with the child is also important.

Another goal of the parent is to ensure that young students get As in all their classes when in elementary school, junior high school, and as close as possible in high school. When Wally Goodwin approached Brian just before high school, he said that Brian needed 1200 or more on his SATs and nearly a straight A average for his grade point average to enter Stanford. While elementary and junior high school was an easy accomplishment, high school was a tough challenge because he was attending one of California's more academic public high schools: University High School in Irvine. Today the school is said to send as many as ten students to Stanford every year because it is so academically tricky. Brian's grade point average was nearly 4.0, and his SAT exceeded 1200 when he took the first test. This allows the admissions office evaluating the athlete to feel confident that the athlete could handle the rigor of Stanford academics.

Preparing for the SATs is an essential part of the puzzle to arriving at Stanford. The SATs in the late 90s were the same as they had been for a very long time, but academic prep schools had learned to teach students to get ready for the test. I had a student who started preparing for the test in the sixth grade and spent years studying vocabulary, math, and reading to score high on the SAT. She aced the test and scored 1600, a perfect score, and she was one of the few students from the high school where I taught that managed to get into Stanford. Because of her experience preparing for the test, she became my son's tutor for several sessions to give him some insight into what he was faced with taking the SAT for the first time. It was imperative to have my son tutored for the SAT, and I would recommend that any student wishing to go to Stanford start preparing for the SAT in the sixth grade and spend the summers gaining knowledge and understanding of the challenging questions asked on that test. I had two students throughout my career as an English teacher who mastered the SAT and scored 1600. Both went to Stanford, and both became outstanding members of the community.

How does a parent keep their child focused on accomplishing nearly a straight A average in high school? It takes a lot of support from the parent to get those straight A's. We helped each of the children to do work for their classes while not doing it ourselves. Papers needed to be typed and organized, and we could save the kids a lot of time by helping with that.

Despite being an English teacher, I never wrote any of my son's or daughter's papers for high school. I made suggestions for organization and typed some documents for them when they were overwhelmed with other work. Both were highly disciplined students and spent extraordinary time working on their homework.

There were also times when difficult reading was challenging for them so we would read the book together. One English teacher in Brian's sophomore year had them read Charles Dickens' *A Tale of Two Cities*. The test was so hard that the student had to identify who the character was that was speaking and to whom they were speaking. The challenge of school kept us busy helping our kids do their best. Therefore, plan on being a tutor to them in high school unless the high school they attend is less academic than University High School.

What is an athletic scholarship but one that is given to the kid because they can handle the academic work at the college? Granted, there are many schools where the academic requirements are less challenging than they are at Stanford. Athletes who attend Stanford must have academic skills because the scholarship is wasted if the student cannot perform the educational work at the college.

The first two years at Stanford include the general education classes that all students take when entering college: history, math, science, and English. These classes are challenging. Tiger Woods once said that succeeding in his courses at Stanford was one of the most significant accomplishments of his career. Tiger attended Western High School in Anaheim, which is not known for its academic prowess, so he walked into Stanford with a tremendous intellectual challenge despite earning excellent grades in high school. As most of us know, he finished just the first two years of college at Stanford before turning pro.

Even though student-athletes who attend Stanford must be academically capable of doing the work, there are majors that athletes are encouraged to take that are less difficult than others. After all, the student-athlete still must have a major and finish it to stay eligible for the four years to perform on the playing field. At the time of my son's Stanford attendance, the major he was encouraged to take was economics. There were a set of courses that were "athlete-friendly," so getting a degree in economics at Stanford was the way to go in his day (2000-2004). Despite that, my son did not major in economics but took a degree in symbolic systems, a cousin to the computer science degree. This was a problematic degree; if he was not working at the golf course, he was working full-time on papers for those courses. He managed to take a very challenging major.

The athletic coach of any team must take his "case" to the admissions department to get their student-athlete into the school. The coach must have players capable of handling the work, so they appeal to the admissions department for approval. That department considers the academic profession the student-athlete has performed in high school. Stanford is aware of the different educational programs of high schools around the country. If they do not know the school, they research it to determine if the challenge at the high school was sufficient to prepare the student for Stanford. To my knowledge, they still require student-athletes to have the highest grades and the best SAT scores so they can manage to handle the rigors of Stanford's academics.

Should a parent have tutors for their student-athlete in high school? Absolutely. If there are complex challenges for the student in high school, then it is best to get support for the student during this schooling period. It is no secret how much time it takes for golfers to make themselves good enough to be asked by the coach to play at Stanford. Stanford has become a premier school where several players have reached the PGA Tour, with the two most notable members being Tiger Woods and Tom Watson. The player has to be very good before being asked by the coach if they want to accept a scholarship to the school. Stanford also recruits from the entire country and around the world for the best players they can get.

Each student-athlete in the time period my son attended Stanford was very good in school. Several of them took the "easy" route academically. However, some took challenging majors that have served them well since graduation. Getting the student-athlete ready to handle the challenges of this school takes a lot of effort on the part of the parents and great motivation on the part of the student. As the reader knows, Brian was motivated in the sixth grade when he learned the name of the college, Stanford. His grit and determination were exercised in his golf and academic life throughout his years in elementary, junior, and high school. Knowing what I knew about the efforts other students were making in my classes is a testimony to his focus on that goal. Let it be that the reader is gifted with a child with so much determination.

Conclusion

"They say golf is like life, but don't believe them. Golf is more complicated than that."

Gardner Dickinson

Getting a golf scholarship to any college is difficult but getting one to Stanford is another level. Exposing kids to sports is one way of determining whether they are athletic enough to take on the challenges of any sport. Golf is a difficult challenge, and it takes a great deal of patience and hard work on the parents' part to make their kids' dreams come true. If you read *Who We Met on the Way to Stanford: A Father's Memoir*, then you will realize the enormous work and challenge of getting there. This has been an effort to show parents of prospective young golfers what is required to prepare the young golfer for the challenges of getting that scholarship.

Just as parents of newborns prepare their child to be an Ivy School graduate, so also are those who want the very best for their kids. Parents need to realize that preparing a child for the world today starts before birth with good nutrition and reading to the child while in the womb.. Parents need to work as hard on the preparation of their child's academics as they do on the practice of the sport of golf. Golf must not be the only sport to play as a child. The child needs to play team sports and know camaraderie among his fellow players. Learning to socialize with others is essential to playing the game of golf in a sporting way.

Parents need to be aware of who best to choose for a golf instructor when the young player is learning and that the time spent is used well. The best golf instructors need to be researched in the nearby community. There are many good instructors, but it is necessary to find a great instructor when the kid is learning the golf swing. Once the head pro at our club saw Brian practicing and he cocked his head as if to say, "What the hell is that?" What the golf club professional did not know was that the golf swing is more round swing than an up and down and that my son was making sure his right hand was on top, coming down into impact. The club pro did not know the more modern swing because he was not up to date with the latest knowledge about the swing. It takes much study of the golf swing to make changes necessary for good ball striking. The golf swing is what gets the ball to the green and then the short game follows. Parents need to be sure that an excellent short game instructor is used when teaching the young golfer proper posture and technique when playing the short game. Outstanding teachers are out there, but research is necessary before committing to anyone. I once had a club pro ask me why I thought I was qualified to teach my son the short game. I told him I had read sixty books on the subject and had a pretty good idea of what to do when chipping and pitching a golf ball. I asked him if he had read three significant books on the subject, and he said he had not. I asked why he didn't know the research of David Pelz in the *Short Game Bible* and the *Putting Bible*? Just because a club pro is a pro does not mean he is a professional who keeps tabs on the knowledge that evolved in his own day about golf. That is the same thing with the golf swing: not all club professionals know the new knowledge about the golf swing.

Learning to practice effectively is quite important to the growth of the player. heWell instructed

Getting to Stanford on a golf scholarship is a mountain to climb, and I hope many of my reader's kids will make it to the top. These have been some of the most useful tips I can think of for the parents to make that happen. All the best in achieving that goal.

Notes

Chapter 1: Early Academic and Athletic Beginnings

Dhuey, et al. "School Age and Cognitive Development."
National Bureau of Economic Affairs. August, 2017.

www.ingramcontent.com/pod-product-compliance
Lightning Source LLC
Chambersburg PA
CBHW071214120626
46546CB00006B/2562